"I read Alex's book and it is brilliant… and quite refreshing. It gives me hope that the things I have been trying to get into schools for four decades will at last find their way into the hands of kids everywhere… Great work!"

Dr Richard Bandler
Co-founder of NLP

"Brilliantly simple and simply brilliant.
Alex's book addresses one of the key issues
facing children and adults alike. If you can't
spell you can't look up the word and you can't connect
it with previously known words. Great job Alex!"

Peter Thomson
The UK's Most Prolific Information Product Creator

First published in Great Britain 2017

by Rethink Press

"Wow! Well done Alex. This book is a must for all children and their parents. It demonstrates that a child who is given a love of learning, the excitement to discover more and a learning strategy that works for him or her, has no limits. I would strongly suggest that teachers read this book and learn from a voracious learner and a young boy with a passion, just how much is possible. This is how all the children in your class can be! Alex is a credit to his Mum Debbie and he is a credit to her."

Kate Benson
International Director of Education for the Society of NLP

"Alex's book has only one flaw... it's extremely frustrating to see someone this talented write such a fantastic book at such a young age. I wish it was me! Really... this book is better than most books on this topic. Alex explains the fantastic spelling strategy in a beautifully simple way. It gets straight to the point, makes it easy to understand and remember and you find yourself making huge changes in how you spell within the first few minutes. Absolutely fantastic work. Alex is a bright young star who can help you to spell. Simply magical."

Owen Fitzpatrick
Psychologist and co-author of 'The Ultimate Introduction to NLP'

"Alex is a phenomenon to be writing, illustrating and publishing a book like this at the age of nine and three quarters. The visual split spelling technique taught in this book is the only guaranteed way to be able to spell complex words in the English language. He makes it look so easy and fun on his delightful YouTube clips. Well done to Alex for wanting to share this wonderful technique to help others gain mastery over English spellings. It's fantastic that he has this desire and passion to help his peers."

Dr Sue Whiting
Grand Master of Memory, former Women's World Memory Champion and author of the 'Wizard of Spells' Magic Memory books.

"Very useful tool for any parent, grandparent or teacher. Giving an insight into how good spellers have learned to spell; whilst teaching you what you can do to more effectively help the young people in your care."

Tina Taylor
Author & Licensed Master Trainer of NLP

"If you've got children it really is a worthy NLP strategy to help them to spell, and if you've not got children - it really is a worthy NLP strategy to help YOU to spell!?!"

Daniel Hill
NLP Master Practitioner

"The aim of Education is to promote and support learning via harnessing an individual's innate ability and metacognition. 'The Secret Spell to Spelling' and the use of NLP within the classroom will prove to be a considerable tool within the reach of all Educational Professionals striving to achieve this."

Mrs Rio Marston
B: ed Hons (University of Birmingham), HNC, ONC

"Is your book on spelling published yet? I tried the technique on my 5 year old and we've got 5 out of 6 right for his test on Thursday. Last week he only got 2 right… and we practised all week for that!"

Michelle Chadderton

"Just read it and I must say it is absolutely brilliant!! You must be so proud, "The Secret Spell To Spelling" Book is a great opportunity for anyone learning to spell. This wonderful method will give you a real boost to accelerate your learning and help make you a dictionary champion. As a parent learning how to spell is one of the most important skills in life. After all learning is the eye of the mind!"

Wendy Ross

"At last an educational book that can be used effectively to help generations to learn how to spell with ease, and best of all it is written by a boy age 9 3/4, a peer from the exact audience that it is designed to help!

My son Rafe is 8 and since we have been using the techniques in the book he not only gets full marks in all of his spelling tests, but he has fun learning them too!

Alex is such an inspiration, it is outstanding to see a young boy so enthusiastic about developing a way of learning that will help so many children excel in an area that may have been a real struggle for them before this book came along. Well done Alex, for taking the initiative and passing on your fantastic idea to help so many. You are a star!"

Julie Saul

"I am so impressed with the book Alex has written, jealous that it is written by a 9 year old and I couldn't do it!

My 7 year old son has embraced it and has gone from 3-4 out of ten in his spelling test on a regular basis to getting 9-10 out of ten in the last 3 weeks. He has learned to spell NECESSARY forwards and backwards and (encouraged by me) has made quite a few pounds betting people he can spell it forwards and backwards.

His confidence levels have soared and his hand writing has improved dramatically.

I think this is the single most important educational tool that I have come across in the 7 years that my kids have been in school and certainly gives more confidence, ability and structure than any of the current methods for spelling the 'education system' are teaching.

With the phonics my son learned he made a sign to go on his bedroom door saying "STOP, noc and if I dont ansar luke for me sumwer alse ales (unless) I am playing hihgd and sece" (hide and seek).

Phonics confuse him and shook his confidence as he couldn't make sense of phonics and phonemes. It is wonderful to see the confidence in him after learning to spell NECESSARY thanks to Alex's methods.

This should be compulsory teaching in schools. It would save so much heartache for those who find phonics confusing."

Simon Lea (Father of 2 very able and intelligent children)

"Alex's book is really helpful, I feel much better at spelling stuff, I feel more confident, my handwriting has improved, and I have loved spelling 'necessary' to everybody because it makes me feel really good that I can do it, and I have managed to get some money by betting people I could spell it - it has been really fun - Thank you Alex."

Jakey Lea (age 7) :)

"This is Perfect! My 9 year old son has loved reading this book. The fact a 9 year old boy is actually reading a book... and a book about spelling and genuinely enjoying it, that is amazing! This has to be a hit!"

Vicki Fisher

"It has helped me with my spellings and now I can spell accompany and accommodate, it is a very interesting book to read and it is very bright, colourful and catchy. The illustrations are amazing and I would definitely recommend it. Alex is an amazing person and I am very proud of him for what he has done - I don't think I could do that!!"

Ollie Lea (age 9)
(winner of the award for literacy out of 60 children and classmate of Alex)

"I found Alex's book very effective in teaching how to spell to learners of English. I showed the book to the head of English and he also said it was great and I should try the method with my students which I have and found it to be very positive."

Ozlem Green
Language Teacher

"Full of epicness! Great book! Helps everyone spell."

Louis Fisher (age 9)

"It is a great book and a flawless way to learn spellings. It has helped me learn supercalifragilisticexpialidocious."

Edward Lealand (age 9)

"When I was at school I really struggled with spelling and it was always a weak point that held me back with my studies. When becoming a parent I then struggled with how my children were taught how to spell and I have given them this book to not only show them another way to spell correctly and effectively but also so that we can learn together. Finally when I found out how much hard work and effort a 9 year old had put into this book it gave me the impulse to try and engage my children into creating something as wonderful as this book."

Tino Schilling (Dad of Two)

"What a wonderful, innovative and fun way for children and adults to learn how to spell. What is even more impressive is how quickly the spelling of my nine year old son has improved using the split method - absolutely fantastic! Do your kids, and yourself, a favour and give this a go."

Phil (Alexander's Dad)

CONTENTS

Let's learn the 'The Secret Spell To Spelling' together with my friends: Özlem, Jake and Olivia...

Özlem   Jake   Olivia   Alex

INTRODUCTION

Hi, I'm Alexander Mole-Williams the author of this book, with a little help from my Mum.

This book is all about a method that helps you to spell any word of your choice.

I call it the Split Method because you split the word into two, three or four chunks. Like this:

NECESSARY   NEC-ESS-ARY

NEC	ESS	ARY

The Split Method is very similar to how we remember a telephone number i.e. 0121 - 234 - 5678. We split the word into bite size pieces for ease of remembering.

THE SECRET SPELL TO SPELLING

It's like magic!

With the 'Secret Spell To Spelling', the extra bit we use is our ability to see in our mind's eye. With practice we lock it in so we can see the word when we need it.

Let's get started:

What you need:

- A4 coloured card cut into four pieces (A6 size).
- A black marker pen.

How you do it:

Find a word that you would like to learn and check it with your dictionary or online for the correct spelling.

- Look at how you can split it up. Do any mini words jump out? i.e TOM-OR-ROW for tomorrow. This will help for remembering. Or you could split them into syllables, i.e.: SAT-UR-DAY.

- Split the word into two, three or more parts if necessary.

- Write each part on a different coloured card. (You can do the words in capitals or lower case.)

- Choose one colour for the start of each word and another for the second part and a third for the third part etc.

- This will help with the games you can play later which will also help you learn the words.

- I use yellow, green then blue.

- Hold the first part of the word up and above your eyes, either to the left, right or centre.

- Sense where you naturally feel you want to hold the card.

- Many are comfortable up and to the left.

- The reason we hold it above eye level is this where we store our visual images and movies in our mind.

Next step of the split method:

- Now imagine your brain is a camera and take a picture in your mind click, click, click as you blink.

- Check that you can see it in your mind.

- See if you can read it forwards and then backwards, if not,

- Re-look at the card and take another mind photo, click, click, click until you can easily see it without the card.

- Then do the same with the other parts of the word, until it's locked in.

- Notice the feeling you feel when you get it right. When you do make sure you get a high five or jump up and down and celebrate.

Once you have done the whole word see if you can spell it forwards and then backwards.

Repeat again and again until you've got it.

The split method is teaching you to store a visual record of the word so that you can easily re-call the photo in mind.

Don't Guess.
It doesn't work and it
can make you unhappy.

After practising with the split method you will become confident spelling words you have learnt as you have captured them in your mind and the feeling 'feels right.'

You are training your brain to create a powerful visual photographic memory, linked with a knowing "you've got it" feeling which will also help you in exams.

You need to practise to really lock it in, but once your mind learns the strategy it can do it much quicker.

Playing games with the cards also helps and is great fun as you are still learning whilst enjoying the game.

Remember my Mum says:
Practice makes perfect and take regular breaks as it's a better way to learn...

"...or you'll go google-eyed!"

This method is also great for tests.

Imagine if you could take photos of the words spelt correctly into the test with you. You could just copy the words and get them all right.

LET'S HAVE SOME FUN

Sometimes big words can be split into smaller words that have a meaning or are easier to remember e.g. the word tomorrow can be split like this:

TOM **OR** **ROW**

Maybe you can think of some of your own words that you can split into smaller words.

We have chosen a few to help you in the following chapters for you to really master this 'Secret Spell To Spelling.'

Practise until you can see them and spell them forwards and backwards and you have a good feeling too...

LET'S GET STARTED

Practise learning some words...

We will start small. Get your coloured card. Pick ten words to learn first - here's some words you might like to choose:

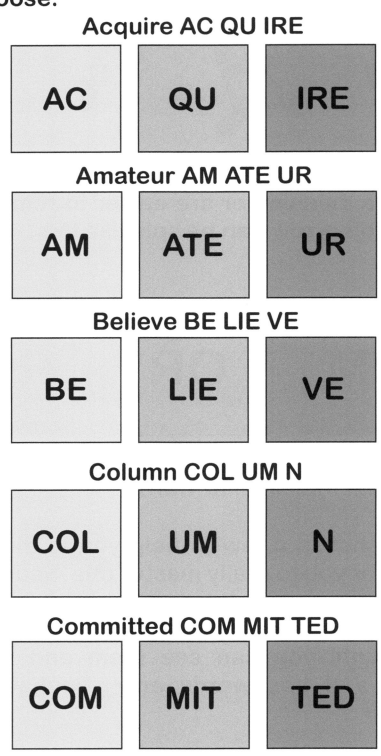

Acquire AC QU IRE

| AC | QU | IRE |

Amateur AM ATE UR

| AM | ATE | UR |

Believe BE LIE VE

| BE | LIE | VE |

Column COL UM N

| COL | UM | N |

Committed COM MIT TED

| COM | MIT | TED |

Circle CIR C LE

CIR	C	LE

Exceed EX CEE D

EX	CEE	D

Egypt EG Y PT

EG	Y	PT

Foreign FOR EIG N

FOR	EIG	N

Friend FRI END
(Splits into two quite nicely)

Fraction FR ACT ION

FR	ACT	ION

Gauge GA U GE

GA	U	GE

Height HE IG HT

HE	IG	HT

Harass HA R ASS

HA	R	ASS

You'll remember the naughty ones!

Illegal ILL E GAL

ILL	E	GAL

Imagine IM AG INE

IM	AG	INE

Inform IN FOR M

IN	FOR	M

January JAN U ARY

JAN	U	ARY

Ketchup KET CH UP

KET	CH	UP

Leisure LE I SURE

LE	I	SURE

Liaison LI AI SON

LI	AI	SON

Library LI BRA RY

LI	BRA	RY

Manoeuvre MANO EU VRE

MANO	EU	VRE

National NAT ION AL

NAT	ION	AL

Opulent OP UL ENT

OP	UL	ENT

Personally PER SON ALLY

PER	SON	ALLY

13

Pyramid PY RAM ID

PY	RAM	ID

Question QUE S TION

QUE	S	TION

Recommend REC OMM END

REC	OMM	END

Square SQ U ARE

SQ	U	ARE

They THE Y

| THE | Y |

Twelfth TW ELF TH

| TW | ELF | TH |

Union UN ION

| UN | ION |

Volcano VOL CAN O

| VOL | CAN | O |

THE GAME

When you have cut out 10 - 15 words and have prasticed learning them, you will have 30 - 45 cards.

You can play this game:

- Two or more can play.

- I like to play with my Mum and Dad.

- Scatter all cards, letters hidden and face down on a flat surface (table or floor).

- Decide who is going to go first (you could throw a dice).

- Take it in turns to turn over 3 cards (to find a word you have learnt to spell).

- You might not do this every time so try to remember the location of letters for when it's your turn again.

- When you find a full word remove it and put it to one side, then have another turn.

- The person who has the most words when all cards have been picked up wins.

This is a great game for all the family to play and helps everyone to spell!

HAVE FUN!

And remember to pass on the
'Secret Spell to Spelling.'

LET'S GO LARGE

MISS	ISSI	PPI

These are some words you might choose to learn:

Absolutely, Acceptable, Accidentally, Accommodate, Accurate, Albuquerque, Apparent, Beginning, Bicycle, Bureau, Category, Challenge, Collaborate, Conscience, Describe, Diarrhoea, Evocable, Exhilarate, Existence, Experience, Fascinate, Fluorescent, Guarantee, Guidance, Happiness, Heroes, Humorous, Ignorance, Immediate, Intelligence, Jealous, Jewellery, Judgement, Knowledge, Laboratory, Length, Lesson, Maintenance, Medieval, Millennium, Mississippi, Necessary, Neither, Occurrence, Original, Perceive, Permanent, Perseverance, Quantity, Quarter, Ridiculous, Repetition, Supersede, Scissors, Science, Sacrilegious, Television, Transparent, Unusual, Usually, Vicious, Village, Wednesday, Welcome, Xylophone, Yachtsman.

40+ MOST MISSPELT WORDS

This gives you a list of the 40+ most misspelt words and how to split them up to spell them correctly.

ACC	UR	ATE

ACCE	PTA	BLE

ADAM	ANT

APP	ARE	NT
BUS	IN	ESS
BEG	INN	ING
CAT	EGO	RY

CRI	TIC	ISE
CONS	CIE	NCE
DEF	INI	TE
DIS	CIP	LINE

EM	BARR	ASS
EQU	IP	MENT
EXIS	TEN	CE
FI	ERY	

FAC	TO	RY
GUA	RAN	TEE
GUI	DAN	CE
HUM	ORO	US

INDI	SPENS	ABLE
INTE	LLIG	ENCE
JUD	GEM	ENT
KNOW	LED	GE

LIC	EN	CE
MISC	HIE	VOUS
MISS	PE	LL
NEI	GHB	OUR

NOTI	CEA	BLE
OCCA	SION	ALLY
OCCU	RRE	NCE
POSS	ESS	ION

PRI	VIL	EGE
PER	SON	NEL
RHY	ME	
RHY	THM	

SCH	EDU	LE
SE	PAR	ATE
TRAN	SPA	RENT
TY	RAN	NY

USU ALL Y

VA CU UM

WE AT HER

WE IR D

HUGE WORDS

Now you've learnt 'The Secret Spell To Spelling' you will be able to split any word you want.

Learn these two and really impress your friends.

Supercalifragilisticexpialidocious

1

SUPER	CALI	FRAG

2

ILIS	TICE	XPIA

3

LIDO	CIO	US

Llanfairpwllgwyngyllgogerychwyrndrobw-lllantysiliogogogoch

This is a town in Wales when translated means:
'The Church of St Mary's in the hollow of the white hazel near the rapid whirlpool at the church of St. Tysilio's by the red cave.'

1

LLAN	FAIR	PWLL

2

GWYN	GYLL	GOGE

3

RYCH	WYRN	DROBW

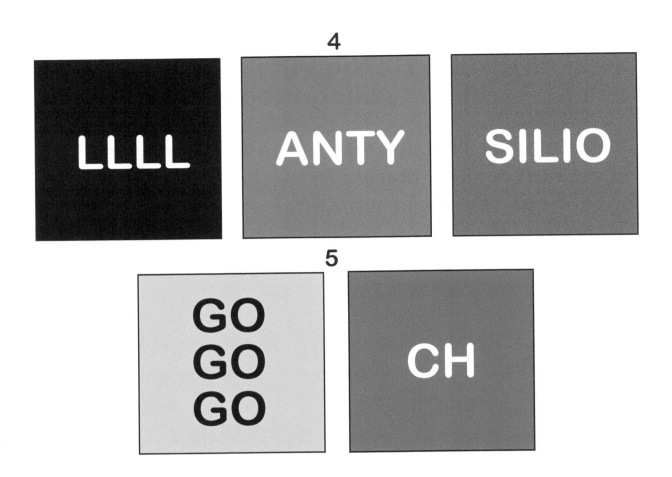

4

LLLL ANTY SILIO

5

GO GO GO CH

The best way to learn this is in short sessions.

Learn the first three parts and then the next three.

Give yourself a break of a day and then come back to learn the next few parts.

Visit 'The Secret Spell To Spelling' You Tube channel to see Mum and I spelling those words forwards and backwards as well as teaching you them.

WORDS THAT SOUND THE SAME

With words that sound the same, connecting them to images can help with remembering the right spelling for the rigth context e.g.

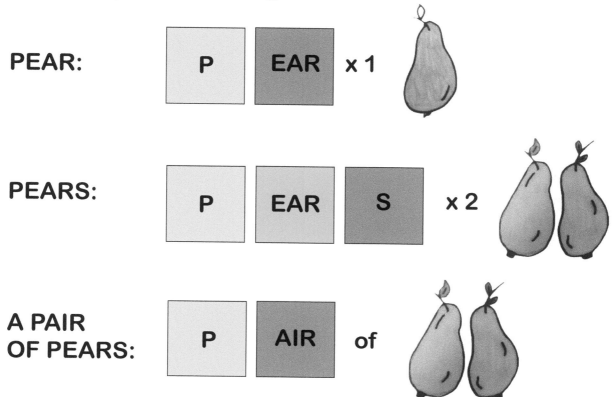

PEAR: | P | EAR | x 1

PEARS: | P | EAR | S | x 2

A PAIR OF PEARS: | P | AIR | of

As you hold up each card to "click, click, click" see if you can add a picture linked to the word to help you remember the different spelling.

PIECE   A   PIE   CE   of PIE

PEACE   World   PEA   CE

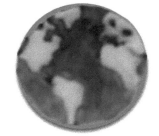 

HEAR   H   EAR

HERE   H   ERE

WRITE | WR | ITE

RIGHT | RI | GHT

NO
RIGHT
TURN

Some words you will just have to learn their meaning by repetition.

THERE | THE | RE | In, at, or to that place or position.

THEIR | THE | IR | Belonging to or associated with people or things.

WHERE | W | HERE | In or to what place or position.

WEAR | W | EAR | Wear an earring in your ear.

Can you think of any more?

FOR DYSLEXIA

I believe this method may be helpful to some dyslexics and also for those who have problems with mastering phonetics at school.

Dyslexics can have great creativity and be lateral thinkers with the ability to think outside the box as well as having great insight.

They can be very determined, empathetic, energetic and fantastic problem solvers.

The word Dyslexia comes from the Greek language and translates to mean a difficulty with words.

Dyslexia is estimated to affect at least 5% of the UK population. It is also believed to run in families.

It is characterised by poor spelling and difficulty decoding and recognising words.

Many dyslexic's experience visual issues of blurred letters, shimmering or shaking letters and words that split into two.

At school, dyslexic children can suddenly realise they are getting left behind with reading and writing and may develop a belief that there is something wrong with them.

THERE IS NOT!

Transparent languages like Spanish, which have a more predictable sound linked with the letters cause fewer problems with dyslexics.

Often these people don't know they are dyslexic as its not been an issue until they attempt to learn English which is not a transparent language.

When you see an 'a' in a word in a transparent language it tends to sound the same in most contexts.

Compared to English, 'a' can take on many different sounds as in apple, wash and Australia.

It must be confusing for children who are trying to make sense of new highly detailed complex rules with lots of exceptions regarding the English language.

YOU CAN LEARN
with the right strategy and practice

There are many famous people who have used the gifts of dyslexia to help them excel in life as they see things differently.

People like; Richard Branson, Steven Speilberg, Alexander Graham Bell, Leonardo da Vinci, Albert Einstein, Lewis Carroll, Tom Cruise, Galileo, Anthony Hopkins, Steve Jobs, Keira Knightly, John Lennon, Jamie Oliver, Nikola Tesla, Holly Willoughby and many more including Alexander Faludy, the yougest Cambridge undergraduate for 200 years.

Imagine what this must feel like to a child?

Imagine suddenly being told to read these weird looking symbols.

Is it Chinese, Japanese or Arabic or even Latin? They don't know. It's all very strange.

They can't get their head around the shapes, let alone their meaning, no matter how hard they try.

They may be concentrating so hard, the words and letters seem to move and jump about which makes it even more difficult to grasp.

They panic and try and get away with it for a while by guessing and bluff their way through, but they are aware everyone else is getting it - but them.

Imagine being shown these weird language symbols called words every day and still not getting it.

They can't run away.

And have to go back.

As they've told themselves they can't do it they shut their mind down to trying.

They feel stressed, worried, and abnormal.

They are starting to dread going to school as they no longer fit in. Their self-esteem plummets and they feel very, very unhappy.

Maybe they show how upset they are with angry outbursts or perhaps they just become very quiet and subdued.

Nothing is fun anymore.

They have been found out to be different and it is scary.

Their identity and self-belief have changed and not for the better.

A Solution?

The split method along with a few well placed hypnotic style suggestions could go a long way to building a bridge to success.

Just like learning a word, to help get a grip on the letters it's better to start small with words like CAT.

Also DOG, BEE and PET are good ones to start with. Plus holding up letters that can be confusing like p, b, d also numbers 6 and 9.

Give each letter a colour, or think of an easy way to remember with an image connected to it, i.e.:

P - Purple
B - Blue
D - Orange

Draw the outline of the letter onto some card and encourage your child to colour them in the colours above.

Then if you cut them out you can add them by clipping them onto the short words with a clothes peg.

With repetition it can help to lock in the shape of the word in the right direction.

Hold the word up and now suggest to your child:

SEE the peg
HOLDING THE WORD IN PLACE
it's KEEPING IT STILL so
YOU CAN EASILY LEARN
to READ IT

Saying certain words slightly louder will work like an embedded command to the child's unconscious mind.

This helps you to help them to build on this Easy Learning Strategy.

Getting your child to help you to draw the letters onto cards helps them to connect to the shape using the kinaesthetic modalities (feelings and touch).

You can draw the word/letter in pencil and then let them trace over it with a felt tip pen for them to copy.

Building a structure in the child's mind of the photograph of the letters and then short words can be a base to build upon.

It will give confidence back to your child as well as a fantastic spelling strategy that can seem like magic.

Please visit my YouTube channel Debbie Williams NLP as I will be recording lots of videos to help with this.

I am always open to suggestions to record more videos that could help your child and others.

Thank you for reading my book
Hope you enjoyed it
Alexander Mole - Williams
With a little help from my Mum
Debbie Williams

MUM'S HYPNOSIS OFFER

Get your free hypnosis and NLP recording by my Mum.

"Stop worrying and create a wonderful life".

What's on it?

1. Develop a photographic memory
2. Unlock the quantum learning machine inside
3. Access the strategies of geniuses
4. Dump your worries to one side for good
5. Learn to work smart not hard
6. Harness your unconscious mind
7. Learn strategies for visualisation
8. Always get a good night's sleep

With my Mum's help on this recording you'll be amazed as problems dissolve into solutions all accomplished through methods Mum has developed through years of intensive study working with hypnotherapy and NLP pioneers.

Mum has worked with Dr Richard Bandler, Paul McKenna, Tony Robbins and Stephen Brooke's of British Hypnosis Research amongst many others.

www.debbiewilliams.co.uk

"Debbie Williams is a Skilled and Effective
NLP Trainer & Hypnotherapist."
Paul McKenna

Dear Alexander,

From the moment you were born, I knew you were special. Choosing to be born 3 weeks early on the 24th February which coincidentally (or not) is Dr Richard Bandler and Tony Robbins birthdate too.

You carry wisdom beyond your years, including chastising me "Mummy, why do you drink wine when you know you will feel bad tomorrow."

You started writing your first books at 6 years old after one day waking up and declaring you were going to write one. You asked about selling it on Amazon and having it printed to look professional and suggesting ways to market it. I couldn't work out where this new focus had come from until I realised you had been listening to my hypnosis recording "Overcome writers block to create a best seller."

From 2 years of age you were obsessed with washing machines. Any outings had to include a visit to an electrical shop so that you could check them out.
You studied the Argos catalogue and knew the name of every single washing machine they sold from Miele to Indesit to Samsung to Tricity Bendix and about 20 more. (And so did we as you taught us).

The local shop nicknamed you their little engineer. I wish I'd recorded a video of you doing your inspection making comments and comparison of each make. Overnight you changed your focus to traffic lights, then lampposts and maps. One Christmas you asked for an A-Z for Birmingham and one of your earlier books created and was a map of a made up town called Coldsbury.

Do you realise son, your dream has come true of having your book published? I've enjoyed working with you on your spelling book immensely, although I've not done very much at all as you've used your weekly Apple computer lessons to learn the skills needed to do the layout for books as well as editing for videos. You are becoming more confident in doing your own videos and you've been asked at school to teach other children your method.

We've seen first hand how children lose their confidence when they can't spell. I hope we will do more videos together to help give children everywhere access to learning how to spell as well as adding ones for managing emotions and building confidence.

You are caring, sensitive, loving, kind and my beautiful little man. My heart bursts with love and pride for you. You know you have been nurtured and loved by all of your family since before you were born.

I hope to carry on teaching you the good values and beliefs my father taught me which have influenced me to this day. Things like, If you can't help someone don't hurt them also success is the greatest revenge and what comes around goes around.

And a few of my own work hard but always look how to work smart by asking questions like; "How can I do this easier, quicker, more effectively and create an outstanding result and enjoy the journey" and "I wonder what miracles will happen today?"

All my love
Mum